TABLE OF CONTENTS

Introduction	4
Using this Workbook	6
Session Outline	8

SESSIONS

Session One: A Strange Choice	10
Session Two: Deeply Driven	28
Session Three: The Best Choice	44
Session Four: Financial Margin	60
Session Five: Sabbath	76
Session Six: Technology	92

APPENDICES

Frequently Asked Questions (FAQ)	110
Small Group Agreement	112
Small Group Calendar	113
Memory Verses	114

SMALL GROUP LEADERS

Prayer and Praise Report	118
Small Group Roster	119
Hosting an Open House	120
Leading for the First Time	121
Leadership Training	122

INTRODUCTION

If you were to ask someone how life is going right now, chances are they would say, "It's busy!" or even, "I'm overwhelmed!" Our culture runs at a frenetic pace, and it tends to pull us into more commitments, demands, and expectations. Deep down, I think most of us wish we could live differently. All of us wish we had more time to deepen important relationships, energy to invest in our biggest priorities, and space to rest in things that replenish and recharge us. But few of us rarely experience these things in a culture running at warp speed.

The truth is we don't have to live this way. Many times we feel like we have to live at a crazy pace, but we actually do have a say in the matter. We can choose to have margin in our lives, where we live below our limit and leave space for unhurried time and unspent resources. This is the way Jesus chose to live His life—and He's offering it to us if we follow Him. It is also a strange choice to make, one that feels foreign to many of us today.

Over the next six weeks, we're going to talk about choosing to have margin and how it could drastically improve our lives in every way. Because this choice isn't common in our culture, it's important that we talk about it with others, which is why I'm so excited about this book. We want to make it as easy as possible for you to gather with a few friends to discuss these different sessions. So, if you haven't already, invite a few others to do this study with you—maybe it's another family member, a co-worker, a neighbor, or someone else. Chances are they, too, are feeling overwhelmed in our busy culture.

We're excited about what God has in store for you over the next six weeks, and we're praying that you will experience God in a fresh way throughout this study.

JEFF JONES
Senior Pastor of
Chase Oaks Church

"Because this choice isn't common in our culture, it's important that we talk about it with others, which is why I'm so excited about this book."

USING THIS WORKBOOK

Tools to help you have a great small group experience.

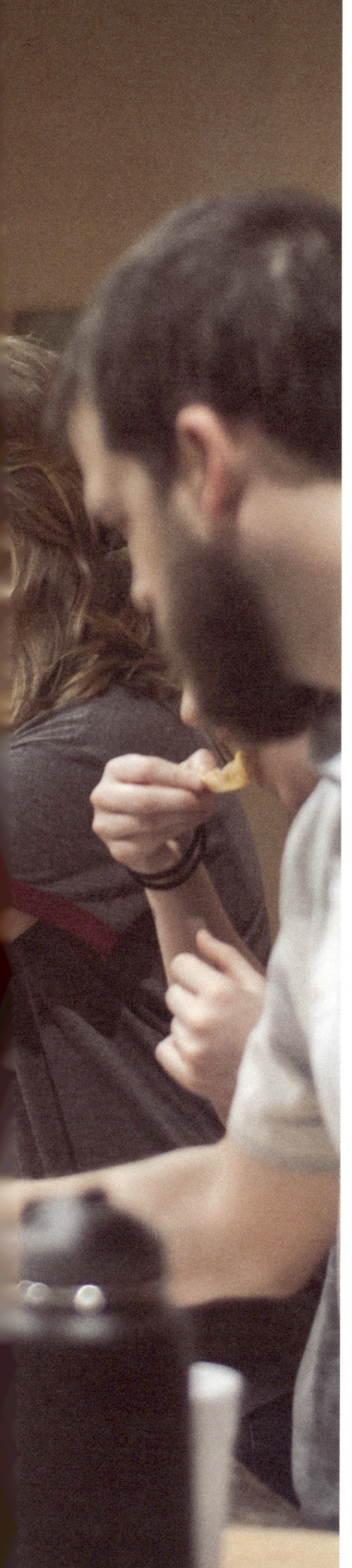

- In the Table of Contents, there are three sections: (1) Sessions; (2) Appendices; and (3) Small Group Leaders. Familiarize yourself with the Appendices. Some of them will be used in the sessions themselves.

- If you are leading or co-leading a small group, the section Small Group Leaders will give you tips for effective leadership, encourage you, and help you avoid a few common obstacles.

- Use this workbook as a guide, not a straitjacket. If the group responds to the lesson in an unexpected but honest way, go with that. If you think of a better question than the one in the lesson, ask it. Take to heart the insights included in the Frequently Asked Questions pages and the Small Group Leaders section.

- Enjoy your small group experience.

- Pray before each session—for your group members, for your time together, and for wisdom and insights.

- Read the Outline for Each Session on the next pages so you understand how the sessions will flow.

SESSION **OUTLINE**

A typical group session for the Margin study will include the following sections. Read through this to get a clear idea of how each group meeting will be structured:

WEEKLY MEMORY VERSES
Each session opens with a Memory Verse that emphasizes an important truth from the session. This is an optional exercise, but we believe memorizing Scripture is a powerful way to grow spiritually. We encourage you to give this important habit a try. The verses for each session are also listed in the Appendix.

INTRODUCTION
Each lesson opens with a brief thought that will help you prepare for the session and get you thinking about that week's topic. Make it a practice to read these before the session. You may want to have the group read them aloud.

SHARE YOUR STORY
The foundation for spiritual growth is an intimate connection with God and His family. You build that connection by sharing your story with a few people who really know you and who earn your trust. This section includes some simple questions to get you talking—letting you share as much or as little of your story as you choose.

HEAR GOD'S STORY
In this section, you'll read the Bible and listen to teaching in order to hear God's story—and begin to see how His story aligns with yours. When the study directs you to, you'll watch a short teaching segment on video. You'll then have an opportunity to read a passage of Scripture and discuss both the teaching and the text. The goal isn't to accumulate information but to apply the insights from the Scripture to your daily life.

STUDY NOTES
This brief section provides additional commentary, background, and insights on the passage you've studied or on some aspect of the video teaching.

CREATE A NEW STORY
In this section, you'll have an opportunity to go beyond Bible study into biblical living. This section will also have a question or two that will challenge you to live out your faith by serving others, sharing your faith, or worshiping God.

FOR ADDITIONAL STUDY

If you have time and want to dig deeper into more Bible passages about the topic, we've provided additional passages and questions. You can use them during the meeting or as homework. Your group may choose to read and prepare before each meeting in order to cover more biblical material. Or group members can use the additional study section during the week after the meeting. If you prefer not to do study homework, this section will provide you with plenty to discuss within the group. These options allow individuals or the whole group to expand their study while still accommodating those who can't do homework or are new to your group.

DAILY DEVOTIONS

Each week on the Daily Devotions pages, we provide Scriptures to reflect on between sessions. This provides you with a chance to slow down, read just a small portion of Scripture each day, and pray through it. You'll then have a chance to journal your response to what you've read. Use this section to seek God on your own throughout the week. During this time, begin and end your Daily Devotion with prayer. Don't rush this process; take your time to hear from God and talk to Him!

A STRANGE CHOICE

Life is so busy. We are busy at work. We are busy at home. We are busy with our family activities. We are busy at church. As a result, most of us feel overstretched when it comes to our time, relationships, and finances. We're trying to keep up with a culture that is running on overdrive all the time. It's no wonder most of us feel stressed and behind, and words like "joy," "rest," and "peace" sound so foreign.

We don't have to live this way. Many times, we feel like we don't have any choice but to live at or above our limits. However, we can choose to live differently. We can decide to have margin in our lives—where we intentionally leave space for things that matter most, for relationships to develop, for money to be left over at the end of the month, and for opportunities to recharge and rest.

This choice is a strange one. Although most of us don't live this way today, margin is a Jesus-like choice. Over the course of the next six weeks, we will look at what this choice looks like and how it has the promise to change the whole trajectory of our lives.

Very early in the morning, while it was still dark, Jesus got up, left the house and went off to a solitary place, where he prayed.
Mark 1:35

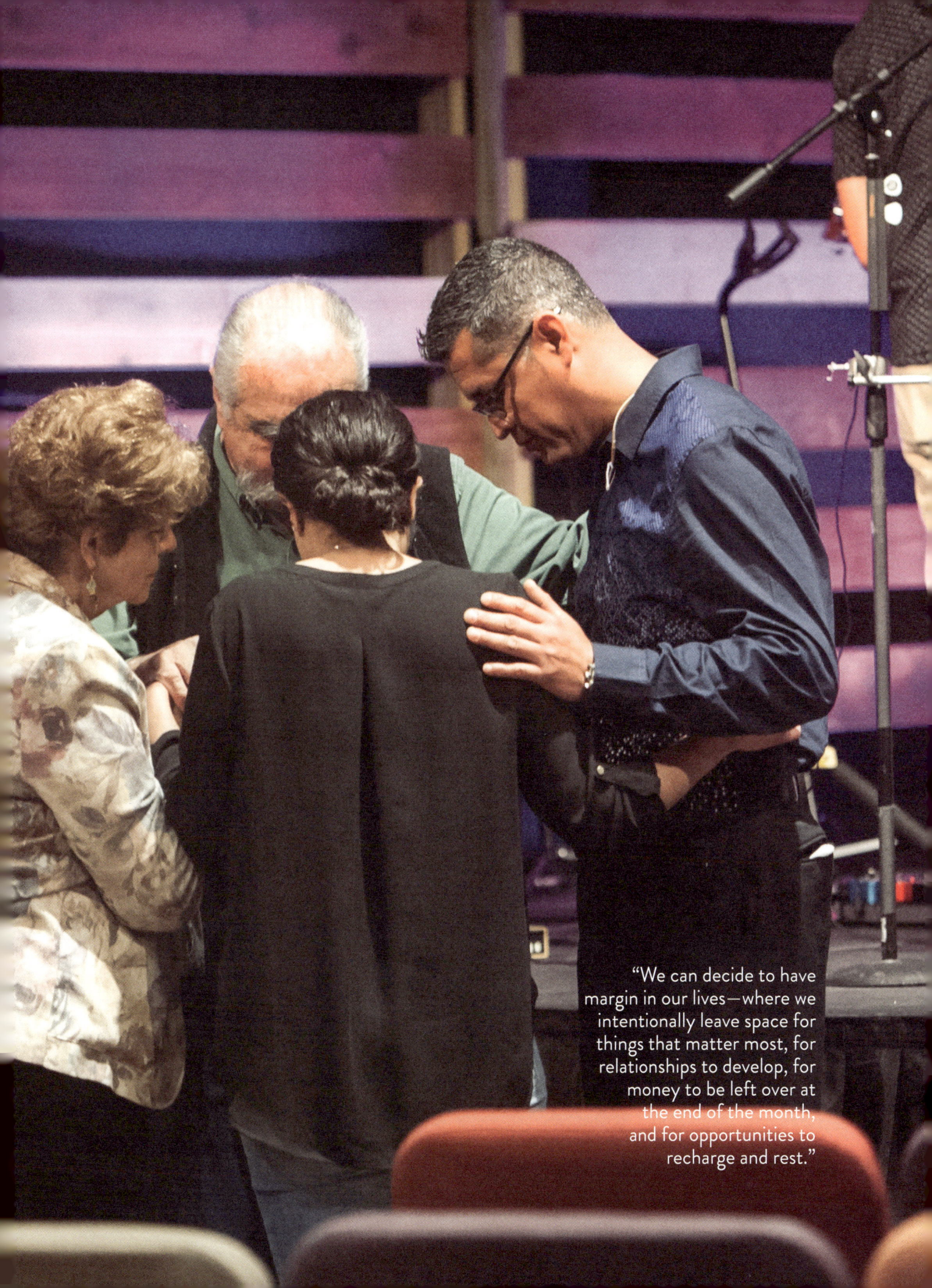

"We can decide to have margin in our lives—where we intentionally leave space for things that matter most, for relationships to develop, for money to be left over at the end of the month, and for opportunities to recharge and rest."

LEADER NOTES

- If your group is new, welcome newcomers. Introduce everyone. You may want to have name tags for this first meeting.

- Open your group with a brief prayer asking God for insight as you study. You can pray for specific requests at the end of the meeting or stop momentarily to pray if a particular situation comes up during discussion.

- Before you start this first meeting, get contact information for every participant. Take time to pass around a copy of the Small Group Roster on page 119 or a blank sheet of paper. Ask someone to make copies or type up a list with everyone's information and email it to the group during the week.

- Whether your group is new or ongoing, it's always important to review your values. On page 112 is a Small Group Agreement with important values for sustaining healthy, balanced groups. Choose one or two of these values—ones you haven't previously focused on or those you have room to grow in—to emphasize during this study.

- The Small Group Calendar on page 113 is a tool for planning who will host and lead each meeting. Consider rotating hosts and leaders, and take a few minutes to plan future meetings.

SHARE YOUR STORY

Begin your time together by using the following questions and activities to get people talking:

- What brought you here? What do you hope to get out of this group?

- On a scale of 1-10, how overwhelming is life right now? Why? What is the biggest source of stress?

WATCH THE VIDEO

Use the space provided to record your thoughts and questions as well as the things you want to remember or follow up on. After watching the video, have someone read the discussion questions in the Hear God's Story section and start the conversation.

HEAR GOD'S STORY

READ MARK 1:35-39

Very early in the morning, while it was still dark, Jesus got up, left the house and went off to a solitary place, where he prayed. Simon and his companions went to look for him, and when they found him, they exclaimed: "Everyone is looking for you!" Jesus replied, "Let us go somewhere else—to the nearby villages—so I can preach there also. That is why I have come." So he traveled throughout Galilee, preaching in their synagogues and driving out demons.

THINK ABOUT IT

- What steps did Jesus take in order to find unhurried time? Make some observations together.

- Is it easy or hard for you to find unhurried time in your day? If you can find it, where or what time of the day does it tend to happen?

- Why did the disciples decide to interrupt Jesus? Put yourself in their shoes—what do you think they expected Jesus to do when they said, "Everyone is looking for you!"?

- Why do you think Jesus responded the way He did? What does it tell you about how He ordered His time, energy, and life?

STUDY NOTES

It is interesting to think that Simon and the other disciples probably would have been happy to stay in Capernaum and observe Jesus teaching and healing the sick every day in the synagogue. Simon almost accusingly said, *"Everyone is looking for you!"* In other words, the disciples were saying, "How could you be so insensitive? Don't you know that the people are looking for you and they have needs?" Jesus' response must have surprised them. He decided to move on to a new location. He knew He wasn't here to meet every need but to extend the Good News further. So they left, even though there were many needs unmet. Jesus knew that He couldn't do it all, and He wasn't going to try. He chose to live well within His limited time.

CREATE A NEW STORY

In this section, talk about how you will apply the wisdom you've learned from the teaching and Bible study. Then think about practical steps you can take in the coming week to live out what you've learned.

- If we know living overworked lives is not great, why do so many of us live this way?

- If you could gain margin in one area of your life (i.e., an extra hour of unhurried time somewhere, an extra amount of money somewhere in your budget, an extra amount of energy in one relationship), where would it be and why?

- What obstacles do you face in creating more margin in your life?

- What is one thing you could do to choose to live with margin somewhere?

- Sometimes, in the middle of the hustle and bustle of life, it's easy to forget something important: the people God has placed all around us. God loves them, and He has placed them in our lives for a reason—to reflect His love to them. So as we slow down our lives a bit during this Margin series, let's think about the people who surround us.

- Take a look at the Circles of Life diagram and write the names of two or three people you know who maybe don't know Jesus. Commit to praying for God's guidance and an opportunity to connect with each of them. Would they be open to joining the group? Share your lists with the group so you can all be praying for the people you've identified.

- This week, how will you interact with the Bible? Can you commit to spending time in the Daily Devotions? Tell the group how you plan to follow Jesus this week, and then, talk about your progress and challenges.

- Give each person an opportunity to share prayer requests.

- If you'd like, you can write these on the Prayer & Praise Report on page 119.

- Close your meeting with prayer.

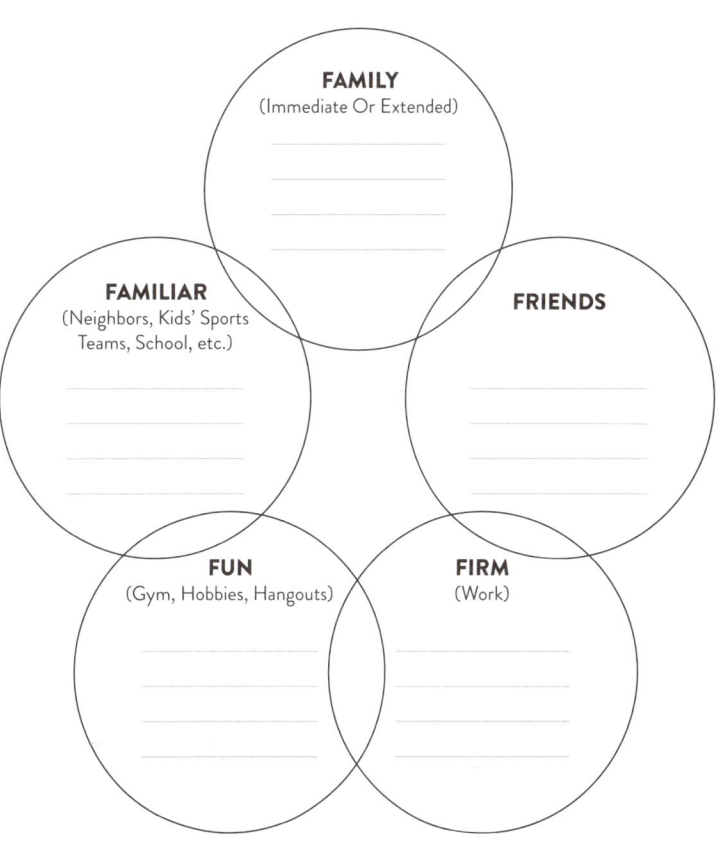

FOR ADDITIONAL STUDY

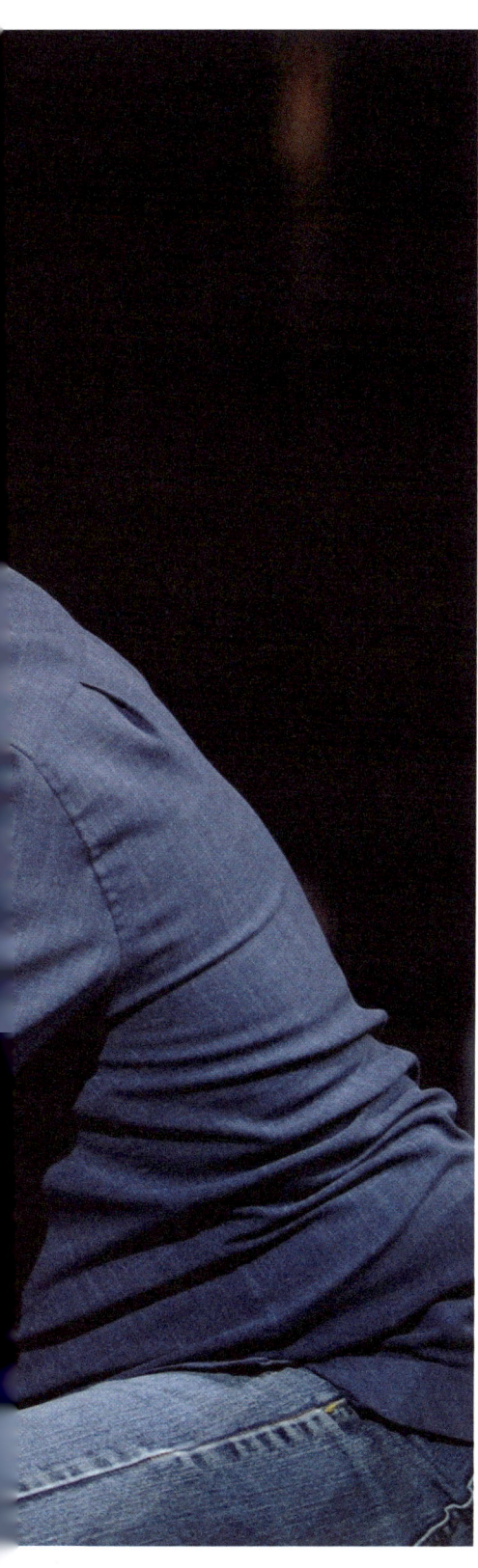

Take some time between now and your next meeting to dig into God's Word. Explore the Bible passages related to this session's theme on your own. Jot down your reflections in a journal or in this study guide. You may want to use a Bible website or app to look up commentary on these passages. If you would like, share what you learn with the group during the next meeting.

READ MATTHEW 6:33

But seek first his kingdom and his righteousness, and all these things will be given to you as well.

- What does it mean to "seek first his kingdom and his righteousness"?
- How do you know if you are truly seeking the kingdom first?
- Do you trust that God will take care of your needs?

READ MATTHEW 6:19-21

Do not store up for yourselves treasures on earth, where moths and vermin destroy, and where thieves break in and steal. But store up for yourselves treasures in heaven, where moths and vermin do not destroy, and where thieves do not break in and steal. For where your treasure is, there your heart will be also.

- How do these verses relate to our study?
- What are earthly treasures that you worry about?
- How can you store up treasures in Heaven?

DAILY DEVOTIONS

DAY 1

MATTHEW 11:28

Come to me, all you who are weary and burdened, and I will give you rest.

REFLECT

When life gets busy, we often forget to recharge by spending time with God, who wants to give us rest and refreshment. What would it look like to rest in Jesus today?

DAY 2

MATTHEW 14:23

After he had dismissed them, he went up on a mountainside by himself to pray. Later that night, he was there alone.

REFLECT

Don't feel guilty about carving out time for yourself. Jesus did it, and so can you.

DAY 3

PSALM 127:2

In vain you rise early and stay up late, toiling for food to eat—for he grants sleep to those he loves.

REFLECT

God wants you to be healthy in every aspect of your life, even your sleep. Are you taking care of your physical needs?

DAY 4

PSALM 1:3

That person is like a tree planted by streams of water, which yields its fruit in season and whose leaf does not wither—whatever they do prospers.

REFLECT

Can you identify with this verse? Why or why not?

DAY 5

2 CORINTHIANS 5:9

So we make it our goal to please him, whether we are at home in the body or away from it.

REFLECT

In a practical way, how can you worship God wherever you are?

DAY 6

REFLECT

Use the following space to reflect on what you learned this week and what God is saying to you.

2
DEEPLY DRIVEN

Almost all of us would say we are busy. But how often do we think about why we are so overloaded? Deep down, there's a part of us that probably likes to be busy—all of us want to feel needed and important.

Within all of us, there are deeper drivers at play that often fuel us to go to the limit or beyond it. If we don't get down below the surface to think about what really drives us, our lives will never change. We may make a few adjustments to a habit or two, but eventually we'll go back into the same patterns that drove us to be busy in the first place.

In this session, let's dig down for an important discussion about why our busyness is often self-imposed.

Whatever you do, work at it with all your heart, as working for the Lord, not for human masters...
Colossians 3:23

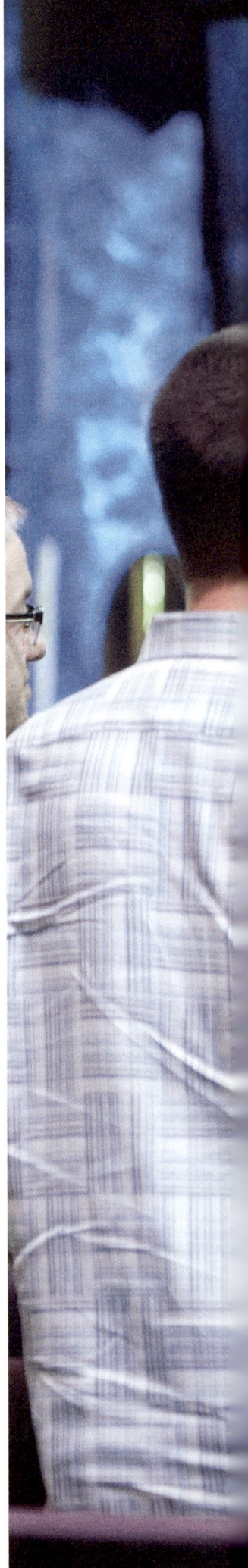

SHARE YOUR STORY

Open your group with a brief prayer asking God for insight as you study. You can pray for specific requests at the end of the meeting, or stop momentarily to pray if a particular situation comes up during your discussion.

- Describe a time where you were really living over your limit. How did life get that way?

- Do you think being busy is sometimes self-imposed—that we choose it because it feels good? In what ways can being busy feel good today?

- In the last session, we asked you to write some names in the Circles of Life diagram. Who did you identify as the people in your life that God has placed in your life? Go back to the Circles of Life diagram on page 23 to help you think of various people you come in contact with on a regular basis; people who need to know Jesus more deeply. Consider ideas for action and make a plan to follow through on one of them this week.

WATCH THE VIDEO

Use the space provided to record your thoughts and questions as well as the things you want to remember or follow up on. After watching the video, have someone read the discussion questions in the Hear God's Story section and start the conversation.

HEAR GOD'S STORY

READ MATTHEW 4:1-11

Then Jesus was led by the Spirit into the wilderness to be tempted by the devil. After fasting forty days and forty nights, he was hungry. The tempter came to him and said, "If you are the Son of God, tell these stones to become bread." Jesus answered, "It is written: 'Man shall not live on bread alone, but on every word that comes from the mouth of God.'" Then the devil took him to the holy city and had him stand on the highest point of the temple. "If you are the Son of God," he said, "throw yourself down. For it is written: "'He will command his angels concerning you, and they will lift you up in their hands, so that you will not strike your foot against a stone.'" Jesus answered him, "It is also written: 'Do not put the Lord your God to the test.'" Again, the devil took him to a very high mountain and showed him all the kingdoms of the world and their splendor. "All this I will give you," he said, "if you will bow down and worship me." Jesus said to him, "Away from me, Satan! For it is written: 'Worship the Lord your God, and serve him only.'" Then the devil left him, and angels came and attended him.

THINK ABOUT IT

- The first temptation was about turning a stone into bread. What did the bread signify for Jesus?

- In the second temptation, Jesus had to choose to trust in God or worry what others might think of Him. Is this a temptation for you?

- The third temptation was about accomplishment. How did Jesus fight off this temptation?

- Why was it so important for Jesus to face these temptations? What did it mean for Jesus' mission that He was able to resist all three temptations?

STUDY NOTES

We all have plenty of temptations in our lives. But the passage on **Matthew 4:1-11** gives us the best tools to fight off temptation. First of all, know the Bible. Jesus fought all the temptations by quoting Scripture. Second, obey God. When you are tempted, remind yourself that you are a child of God and that you want to obey your Father in Heaven. Third, don't look for your purpose by trying to satisfy your flesh. Instead, focus on the mission that God has given to you.

CREATE A NEW STORY

In this section, talk about how you will apply the wisdom you've learned from the teaching and Bible study. Then think about practical steps you can take in the coming week to live out what you've learned.

- Within all of us, there can be deeper drivers that often drive us to live overfull lives. Maybe it is gaining more material possessions, accomplishing big things, or getting the attention of other people. Which of these deeper motives tend to drive you off course? Why?

- Are these inner drivers always bad? How do you know when a desire for achievement or accomplishment gets out-of-whack?

- What changes do you need to make in order to confront these deeper drivers and create more margin in your life?

- Spend time with God. It's a great way to reorient our lives and confront the deepest drivers in our lives.

Here are some simple ways to connect with God. Tell the group which ones you plan to try this week, and then talk about your progress and challenges when you meet next time.

- Commit to personal prayer and daily connection with God. You may find it helpful to write your prayers in a journal.

- Do the Daily Devotions provided in each session. It's an opportunity to read a short Bible passage five days a week during the course of our study. Take time to read carefully and reflect on the passage. Write down your insights about what you read each day. Copy a portion of Scripture on a card and tape it somewhere in your line of sight, such as your car's dashboard or the bathroom mirror. Or text it to yourself! Think about it when you sit at red lights or while you're eating a meal. Reflect on what God is saying to you through these words. On the sixth day, summarize what God has shown you throughout the week.

- Give each person an opportunity to share prayer requests. If you'd like, you can write these on the Prayer and Praise Report on page 118.

- Close your meeting with prayer.

FOR ADDITIONAL STUDY

Take some time between now and your next meeting to dig into God's Word. Explore the Bible passages related to this session's theme on your own. Jot down your reflections in a journal or in this study guide. You may want to use a Bible website or app to look up commentary on these passages. If you would like, share what you learn with the group during your next meeting.

READ ROMANS 14:8

If we live, we live for the Lord; and if we die, we die for the Lord. So, whether we live or die, we belong to the Lord.

- What do you think when reading this verse?

- Be honest with yourself—who do you live for: God or people?

- What does it look like to live for the Lord? Be specific.

READ LUKE 10:38-42

As Jesus and his disciples were on their way, he came to a village where a woman named Martha opened her home to him. She had a sister called Mary, who sat at the Lord's feet listening to what he said. But Martha was distracted by all the preparations that had to be made. She came to him and asked, "Lord, don't you care that my sister has left me to do the work by myself? Tell her to help me!" "Martha, Martha," the Lord answered, "you are worried and upset about many things, but few things are needed—or indeed only one. Mary has chosen what is better, and it will not be taken away from her."

- What was Martha's priority? And what was Mary's priority?

- Why was sitting at Jesus' feet the right thing to do? Is this living within the margin?

- Is it bad to give in to the pressures of life like Martha did?

DAILY DEVOTIONS

DAY 1

PHILIPPIANS 1:20

I eagerly expect and hope that I will in no way be ashamed, but will have sufficient courage so that now as always Christ will be exalted in my body, whether by life or by death.

REFLECT

What does it look like in your own life to let God be in the driver's seat? Is your hope in Christ? And do you have courage to honor Him in everything you do?

DAY 2

ISAIAH 40:31

...but those who hope in the Lord will renew their strength. They will soar on wings like eagles; they will run and not grow weary, they will walk and not be faint.

REFLECT

God is the Creator of this world. What does this mean for you personally? Are there times you forget that God is the Creator? Why? How can you remind yourself that God is in control?

DAY 3

JOHN 16:33

I have told you these things, so that in me you may have peace. In this world you will have trouble. But take heart! I have overcome the world.

REFLECT

Life is overwhelming enough; find time to rest in God and receive the peace that He has for you.

DAY 4

2 TIMOTHY 1:7

For the Spirit God gave us does not make us timid, but gives us power, love and self-discipline.

REFLECT

When we let the Spirit of God drive us, we receive power, love, and self-discipline. Have you ever experienced this?

DAY 5

1 PETER 5:7

Cast all your anxiety on him because he cares for you.

REFLECT

Don't worry about pleasing others or about getting recognized for your achievements, but rather, put aside your anxiety and trust that God is all you need.

DAY 6

REFLECT

Use the following space to reflect on what you learned this week and what God is saying to you.

3
THE BEST CHOICE

It's difficult to say "no." Saying "yes" feels so much better! But every "yes" comes with a cost, which means we need to think through whether we are agreeing to the best things in life.

Our "yeses" have the potential of getting in the way—if we're not careful, they can start to squeeze out things that are most important to us, including our relationships.

Relationships never go deep when we are moving too fast. Relational depth only happens slowly, including our relationship with God and our relationships with others.

This session, let's talk about the art of saying "no" so that we can say "yes" to spending unhurried time with those closest to us.

The Lord will guide you always; he will satisfy your needs in a sun-scorched land and will strengthen your frame. You will be like a well-watered garden, like a spring whose waters never fail.
Isaiah 58:11

"Every 'yes' comes with a cost, which means we need to think through whether we are agreeing to the best things in life."

SHARE YOUR STORY

Open your group with a brief prayer asking God for insight as you study. You can pray for specific requests at the end of the meeting, or stop momentarily to pray if a particular situation comes up during your discussion. Then begin your time together by using the following questions and activities to get people talking:

- Is it hard for you to say "no"? Why or why not?

- Has it been a struggle to find time for key relationships in your life? What makes it difficult to spend unhurried time with close friends or family?

WATCH THE VIDEO

Use the space provided to record your thoughts and questions as well as the things you want to remember or follow up on. After watching the video, have someone read the discussion questions in the Hear God's Story section and start the conversation.

READ MARK 6:31-32

Then, because so many people were coming and going that they did not even have a chance to eat, he said to them, "Come with me by yourselves to a quiet place and get some rest." So they went away by themselves in a boat to a solitary place.

THINK ABOUT IT

- Describe the situation Jesus and the disciples found themselves in. What words capture their day? Can you identify with what they were experiencing?

- What did Jesus say "yes" to? What choice did He make to create margin, and who did He create margin with?

- What did Jesus say "no" to?

STUDY **NOTES**

The Bible is full of examples of how important solitude and silence was for Jesus. (For example, **Mark 1:12, Mark 1:35, Mark 3:7, Mark 6:46**.) Considering all the times that Jesus withdrew to be alone and pray in quiet places, it's fascinating that as His followers, we still haven't quite figured out how to embrace solitude and silence. It came so naturally to Jesus, but for most of us, it is real work to carve out time alone to pray. Let's work harder on imitating Jesus: *"Jesus often withdrew to lonely places and prayed."* (**Luke 5:16**).

CREATE A NEW STORY

In this section, talk about how you will apply the wisdom you've learned from the teaching and Bible study. Then think about practical steps you can take in the coming week to live out what you've learned.

- Jeff shared how relationships never go deep when we are moving too quickly. Can you identify with that? Describe a relationship that greatly benefited from spending a significant amount of unhurried time—like going on a trip, rooming together, or something else.

- Jesus made time for His closest friends and His relationship with God the Father. What relationships in your life do you most need to make time for?

- How easy is it for you to find time to spend with God? When do you tend to connect with Him most?

- Have you set up any traditions, rules, or rhythms to help you slow down and spend time with those close to you?

- What steps will you take this week to grow in your relationship with God? If you've focused on prayer in past weeks, maybe you'll want to direct your attention to Scripture this week. If you've been reading God's Word consistently, perhaps you'll want to take it deeper and try memorizing a verse. Tell the group what you plan to try this week, and talk about your progress and challenges when you meet next time.

- Give each person an opportunity to share prayer requests. If you'd like, you can write these on the Prayer and Praise Report on page 118.

- Close your meeting with prayer.

FOR ADDITIONAL STUDY

READ JUDGES 7:1-8

Early in the morning, Jerub-Baal (that is, Gideon) and all his men camped at the spring of Harod. The camp of Midian was north of them in the valley near the hill of Moreh. The Lord said to Gideon, "You have too many men. I cannot deliver Midian into their hands, or Israel would boast against me, 'My own strength has saved me.' Now announce to the army, 'Anyone who trembles with fear may turn back and leave Mount Gilead.'" So twenty-two thousand men left, while ten thousand remained. But the Lord said to Gideon, "There are still too many men. Take them down to the water, and I will thin them out for you there. If I say, 'This one shall go with you,' he shall go; but if I say, 'This one shall not go with you,' he shall not go." So Gideon took the men down to the water. There the Lord told him, "Separate those who lap the water with their tongues as a dog laps from those who kneel down to drink." Three hundred of them drank from cupped hands, lapping like dogs. All the rest got down on their knees to drink. The Lord said to Gideon, "With the three hundred men that lapped I will save you and give the Midianites into your hands. Let all the others go home." So Gideon sent the rest of the Israelites home but kept the three hundred, who took over the provisions and trumpets of the others.

- What does this story teach you about making good choices?
- Do you have enough faith to trust in God's guidance?
- Why was God concerned about the Israelites boasting?
- Do you find God encouraging in this passage? Why or why not?

READ DEUTERONOMY 14:2

...for you are a people holy to the Lord your God. Out of all the peoples on the face of the earth, the Lord has chosen you to be his treasured possession.

- What does it mean to be God's holy people?
- What is the significance of being the Lord's treasured possession?
- What is your job as God's treasured possession?

DAILY DEVOTIONS

DAY 1

1 THESSALONIANS 5:16-18

Rejoice always, pray continually, give thanks in all circumstances; for this is God's will for you in Christ Jesus.

REFLECT

Take some time to check on your heart. Are you making time to pray? Are you giving thanks to God? Are you rejoicing in God?

DAY 2

PSALM 111:10

The fear of the Lord is the beginning of wisdom; all who follow his precepts have good understanding. To him belongs eternal praise.

REFLECT

Re-write this verse in your own words and meditate on it.

DAY 3

PSALM 39:6

Surely everyone goes around like a mere phantom; in vain they rush about, heaping up wealth without knowing whose it will finally be.

REFLECT

How do you live your life for the Lord? Be specific.

DAY 4

PROVERBS 16:2

All a person's ways seem pure to them, but motives are weighed by the Lord.

REFLECT

Always search your heart and make sure your motives are honoring God.

DAY 5

ECCLESIASTES 3:1

There is a time for everything, and a season for every activity under the heavens.

REFLECT

What do you need to prioritize during this season of life? Who do you need to spend time with? And what do you need to cut out?

DAY 6

REFLECT

Use the following space to reflect on what you learned this week and what God is saying to you.

FINANCIAL MARGIN

Nowhere do we feel the stress of a margin-less life more than in the area of money. Most of us live right up to (and even over) the limits of our budget. While it might be the American way, it is also a stressful way to live, especially when an unexpected cost comes our way and our homes or cars start falling apart.

The Bible points to a better way: to leave financial margin in our budgets. Wise people make a radical choice to live on less than what they make so they can save and give generously. While living this way is incredibly beneficial, it does require some hard choices. In this session, let's talk practically about how to create financial margin in our lives.

The wise store up choice food and olive oil, but fools gulp theirs down.
Proverbs 21:20

"Wise people make a radical choice to live on less than what they make so they can save and give generously."

SHARE YOUR STORY

Open your group with a brief prayer asking God for insight as you study. You can pray for specific requests at the end of the meeting, or stop momentarily to pray if a particular situation comes up during your discussion. Then begin your time together by using the following questions and activities to get people talking:

- Why do so many of us live at, or above, our financial limit? What pressures exist today that cause us to overextend our budgets?

- How can you relate to the stress of having no financial margin?

- Take some time for each person to share about how they're doing on the challenge of inviting the people on the Circles of Life to church or your small group. What specific conversations are you praying about for the weeks to come?

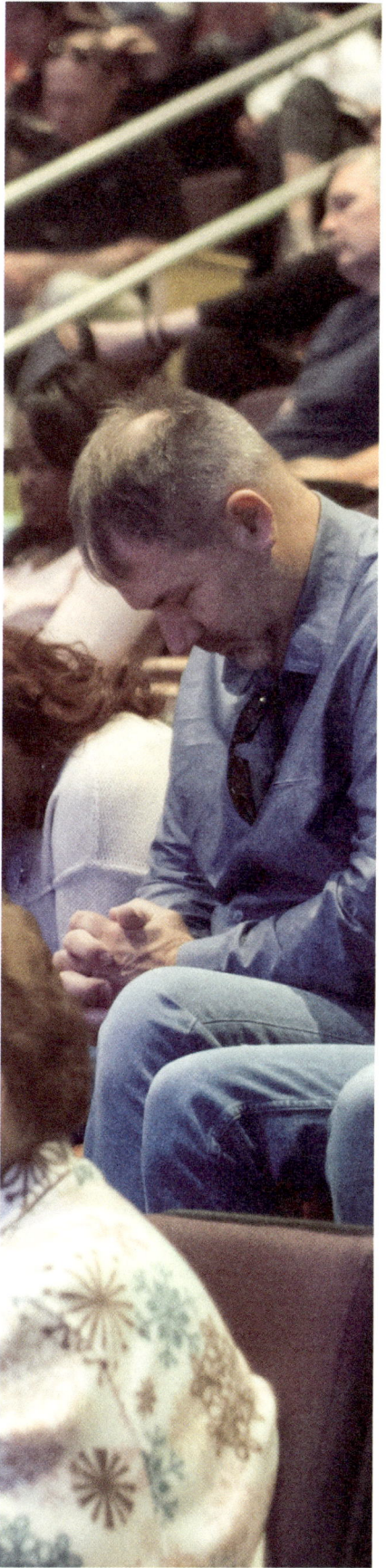

WATCH THE VIDEO

Use the space provided to record your thoughts and questions as well as the things you want to remember or follow up on. After watching the video, have someone read the discussion questions in the Hear God's Story section and start the conversation.

ECCLESIASTES 5:10

Whoever loves money never has enough; whoever loves wealth is never satisfied with their income. This too is meaningless.

PROVERBS 5:10

The plans of the diligent lead to profit as surely as haste leads to poverty.

LUKE 6:38

Give, and it will be given to you. A good measure, pressed down, shaken together and running over, will be poured into your lap. For with the measure you use, it will be measured to you.

THINK ABOUT IT

- What does it mean that people who love money never have enough?
- How can haste lead to poverty?
- Why is generosity so important? What happens when we build our lives around generosity?

STUDY **NOTES**

How can we be wise and diligent with our money? Think of our use of money with three buckets labeled "Give," "Save," and "Live." Before we spend anything, we set aside a percentage to "Give," which is a biblical command—to build our budget around giving and generosity. We also set aside a percentage to "Save," and then live on the rest. Think about it: when we do that, we aren't likely to get into significant financial trouble because we'll have savings to cover us when we have a financial downturn or unexpected expense. Also, we aren't as likely to get into financial trouble because when we build our budget around generosity, we invite God's help into our financial lives.

CREATE A NEW STORY

In this section, talk about how you will apply the wisdom you've learned from the teaching and Bible study. Then think about practical steps you can take in the coming week to live out what you've learned.

- What challenges have you had in building and keeping to a financial plan?

- How are you working at creating financial margin in your life right now? Are you going by the 10/10/80 plan described by Jeff?

- How have you seen God work in your life when you chose to be generous?

- Generosity isn't just about money. We all have different gifts and abilities, and every small group has jobs that need to be done. How could you serve this group—perhaps with hospitality or prayer, by organizing an event researching a topic, or by inviting new people?

- Spend some time praying about those you know who might respond to a simple invitation: to come to a church service, to join your small group, or even to just have coffee and talk about spiritual matters. Ask the Holy Spirit to bring to mind people you can pray for.

- Groups grow closer when they serve together. How could your group serve someone in need? You may want to visit a shut-in from your church, provide a meal for a family who is going through a difficult time, or give other practical help to someone in need. If nothing comes to mind, spend some group time praying and asking God to show you who needs your help. Have two or three group members organize a service project for the group, and then do it!

FOR ADDITIONAL STUDY

Take some time between now and your next meeting to dig into God's Word. Explore the Bible passages related to this session's theme on your own. Jot down your reflections in a journal or in this study guide. You may want to use a Bible website or app to look up commentary on these passages. If you would like, share what you learn with the group during your next meeting.

READ MALACHI 3:10

Bring the whole tithe into the storehouse, that there may be food in my house. Test me in this," says the Lord Almighty, "and see if I will not throw open the floodgates of heaven and pour out so much blessing that there will not be room enough to store it.

- What is a tithe?
- What does it mean *"and see if I will not throw open the floodgates of heaven and pour out so much blessing that there will not be room enough to store it"*?
- Have you ever experienced God's blessing because of your tithing?

READ ROMANS 13:8

Let no debt remain outstanding, except the continuing debt to love one another, for whoever loves others has fulfilled the law.

- What does it mean *"let no debt remain outstanding"*?
- What if we have debts?
- As Christ-followers, what kind of debt do we all have?

DAILY DEVOTIONS

DAY 1

PHILIPPIANS 4:19

And my God will meet all your needs according to the riches of his glory in Christ Jesus.

REFLECT

How have you experienced God meeting your needs? If you haven't experienced this, do you believe God can meet you exactly where you are?

DAY 2

1 TIMOTHY 6:10

For the love of money is a root of all kinds of evil. Some people, eager for money, have wandered from the faith and pierced themselves with many griefs.

REFLECT

What does this verse mean? Is money evil? What is the temptation of money?

DAY 3

PROVERBS 13:11

Dishonest money dwindles away, but whoever gathers money little by little makes it grow.

REFLECT

Have you ever been dishonest when handling your finances? What does it mean to grow money?

DAY 4

MATTHEW 19:21

Jesus answered, "If you want to be perfect, go, sell your possessions and give to the poor, and you will have treasure in heaven. Then come, follow me."

REFLECT

Why did Jesus say this? Look at **Matthew 19:16-19** for context. Why was it so important for the young man to sell his possessions? And what kind of treasure is there in Heaven?

DAY 5

HEBREWS 13:5

Keep your lives free from the love of money and be content with what you have, because God has said, "Never will I leave you; never will I forsake you."

REFLECT

What does a life *"free from the love of money"* look like? Are you content with what you have? Why or why not?

DAY 6

REFLECT

Use the following space to reflect on what you learned this week and what God is saying to you.

SABBATH

None of us were created to work all the time. It's not healthy nor is it effective. Countless research studies have backed up how the best leaders and biggest difference makers take a regular day completely off in order to do something replenishing. They make a decision to create margin and live at a pace below their limits.

The idea of finding a day of rest isn't new. It actually began with a biblical concept known as the Sabbath and is one of the Ten Commandments in the Bible. While God clearly calls us to take rest seriously, this commandment is one we tend to blow off the most.

In this session, let's talk about a simple, yet very counter-cultural choice to take intentional time to rest, replenish, and recharge. The Sabbath may have been a great idea a thousand years ago, but is it possible today?

Remember the Sabbath day
by keeping it holy.
Exodus 20:8

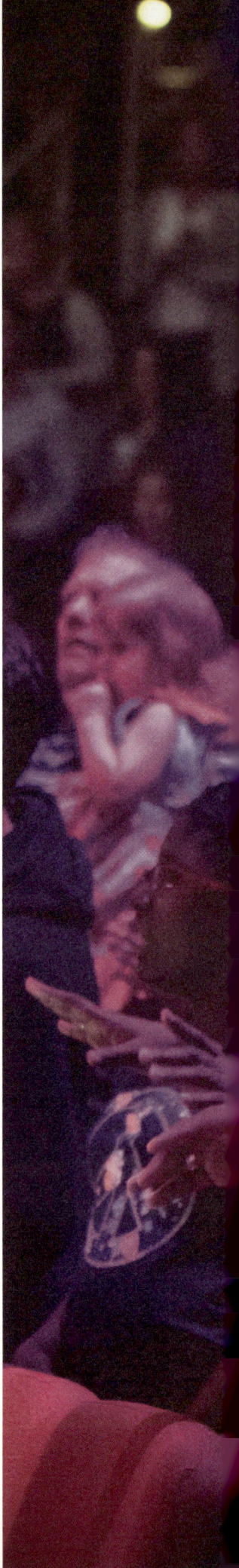

"The best leaders and biggest difference makers take a regular day completely off in order to do something replenishing."

SHARE YOUR STORY

Open your group with a brief prayer asking God for insight as you study. You can pray for specific requests at the end of the meeting, or stop momentarily to pray if a particular situation comes up during your discussion. Then begin your time together by using the following questions and activities to get people talking:

- What did your Sunday routine look like growing up? Did your family talk about or try to honor the Sabbath?

- When was the last time you felt truly rested and replenished? Where was it? What were you doing (or not doing)?

WATCH THE VIDEO

Use the space provided to record your thoughts and questions as well as the things you want to remember or follow up on. After watching the video, have someone read the discussion questions in the Hear God's Story section and start the conversation.

HEAR GOD'S STORY

EXODUS 20:8-11

Remember the Sabbath day by keeping it holy. Six days you shall labor and do all your work, but the seventh day is a sabbath to the Lord your God. On it you shall not do any work, neither you, nor your son or daughter, nor your male or female servant, nor your animals, nor any foreigner residing in your towns. For in six days the Lord made the heavens and the earth, the sea, and all that is in them, but he rested on the seventh day. Therefore the Lord blessed the Sabbath day and made it holy.

MARK 2:23-28

One Sabbath Jesus was going through the grainfields, and as his disciples walked along, they began to pick some heads of grain. The Pharisees said to him, "Look, why are they doing what is unlawful on the Sabbath?" He answered, "Have you never read what David did when he and his companions were hungry and in need? In the days of Abiathar the high priest, he entered the house of God and ate the consecrated bread, which is lawful only for priests to eat. And he also gave some to his companions." Then he said to them, "The Sabbath was made for man, not man for the Sabbath. So the Son of Man is Lord even of the Sabbath."

THINK ABOUT IT

- What does it mean to keep the Sabbath day holy?
- Why did God create the Sabbath?
- How did the Pharisees' idea of the Sabbath differ from Jesus' approach to the Sabbath?

STUDY NOTES

It is mentioned several times in the Bible that the Sabbath is to be kept holy. The Hebrew word for "holy" stands for several things, including clean, sanctify, hallow, dedicate, and consecrate. So when the Bible says to keep the Sabbath holy, it means to set apart the Sabbath from the other six days. It means to honor the Sabbath, to keep it pure, and to dedicate it to our Lord. With this said, let's not forget what Jesus said, *"The Sabbath was made for man, not man for the Sabbath."* (**Mark 2:27**). We are not to treat the Sabbath legalistically, but rather, we need to remember that God created the Sabbath for us, so we can rest.

CREATE A NEW STORY

In this section, talk about how you will apply the wisdom you've learned from the teaching and Bible study. Then think about practical steps you can take in the coming week to live out what you've learned.

- Does the idea of taking an entire day of rest or rejuvenation seem possible for you? Why or why not?

- What is the cost of ignoring rest and rejuvenation? Is there a specific place in your life where you know you are less effective because your tank is empty?

- What is most replenishing and rejuvenating to you?

- Are you intentional about planning time for these activities?

- Jeff said, "No one will do this for us—no one will make sure we're getting time to rest." How can you intentionally plan to rest? How can you get creative about finding Sabbath time?

- A strong group is made up of people who are all being filled up by God so that they are empowered to love one another. What specific steps will you take this week to connect with God privately so He can "fill you up"? If you've focused on prayer in past weeks, maybe you'll want to direct your attention to Scripture this week. If you've been reading God's Word consistently, perhaps you'll want to take it deeper and try memorizing a verse. Tell the group what you plan to try this week and share your progress and your challenges at the next meeting.

- Give each person an opportunity to share prayer requests. If you'd like, you can write these on the Prayer and Praise Report on page 118.

- Close your meeting with prayer.

FOR ADDITIONAL STUDY

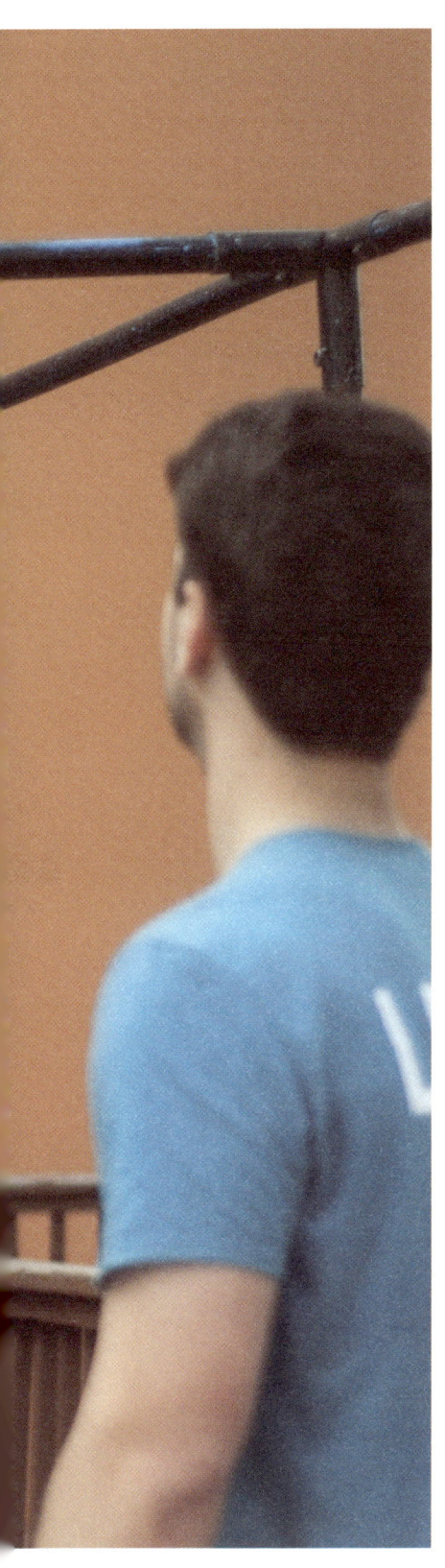

Take some time between now and your next meeting to dig into God's Word. Explore the Bible passages related to this session's theme on your own. Jot down your reflections in a journal or in this study guide. You may want to use a Bible website or app to look up commentary on these passages. If you would like, share what you learn with the group during your next meeting.

READ ISAIAH 58:13

If you keep your feet from breaking the Sabbath and from doing as you please on my holy day, if you call the Sabbath a delight and the Lord's holy day honorable, and if you honor it by not going your own way and not doing as you please or speaking idle words...

- In your own words, what does this verse mean?

- Whose day is the Sabbath?

- What are we supposed to do on the Sabbath? What are we not to do?

EXODUS 31:15-17

For six days work is to be done, but the seventh day is a day of Sabbath rest, holy to the Lord. Whoever does any work on the Sabbath day is to be put to death. The Israelites are to observe the Sabbath, celebrating it for the generations to come as a lasting covenant. It will be a sign between me and the Israelites forever, for in six days the Lord made the heavens and the earth, and on the seventh day he rested and was refreshed.

- What does the Sabbath signify?

- What do we need to rest from on the Sabbath? Look at your everyday life and try to be as specific as possible.

- When you keep the Sabbath, do you feel refreshed?

- Ask God where you are too busy and need rest.

DAILY DEVOTIONS

DAY 1

ISAIAH 56:2

Blessed is the one who does this—the person who holds it fast, who keeps the Sabbath without desecrating it, and keeps their hands from doing any evil.

REFLECT

To keep the Sabbath is to embrace God's law. Are you obedient to God? If not, what hinders you?

DAY 2

MARK 2:27

Then Jesus said to them, "The Sabbath was made for man, not man for the Sabbath."

REFLECT

What did Jesus mean when He said that the Sabbath was made for people and not the other way around?

DAY 3

HEBREWS 4:9-11

There remains, then, a Sabbath-rest for the people of God; for anyone who enters God's rest also rests from their works, just as God did from his. Let us, therefore, make every effort to enter that rest, so that no one will perish by following their example of disobedience.

REFLECT

To rest is to obey. Why do you think we need to be told to rest? What does God know about us that He would make such a commandment?

DAY 4

LUKE 23:56

Then they went home and prepared spices and perfumes. But they rested on the Sabbath in obedience to the commandment.

REFLECT

What can you do leading up to your Sabbath so that you can rest and enjoy the Sabbath to its fullest?

DAY 5

MATTHEW 12:12

How much more valuable is a person than a sheep! Therefore it is lawful to do good on the Sabbath.

REFLECT

Honor the Sabbath, but honor the one who created the Sabbath even more.

DAY 6

REFLECT

Use the following space to reflect on what you learned this week and what God is saying to you.

6

TECHNOLOGY

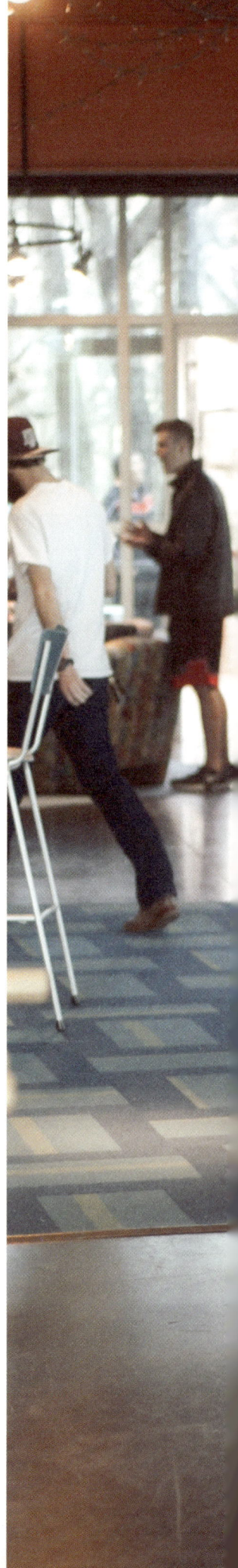

Technology is everywhere. Most of us carry a phone in our pocket that is more powerful than computers were ten years ago. Technology is truly remarkable—we can listen to new music, connect with far-away friends, and access any type of information. And most of us get lost a lot less thanks to our handy maps apps.

While technology can be extremely helpful, it also makes living a life with margin challenging. Our daily life is full of buzzes and rings that alert us to something that is noteworthy or requires our attention. In countless ways, our lives are easier because of technology, but are they better and more joyful? Are we fully present when we need to be, or are we living more distracted because of it?

In this final session, let's get very practical and talk about something that is all around us and fills up much of our day. Let's consider how to find margin in a technology-saturated world.

I press on toward the goal to win the prize for which God has called me heavenward in Christ Jesus.
Philippians 3:14

"While technology can be extremely helpful, it also makes living a life with margin challenging."

SHARE YOUR STORY

Open your group with a brief prayer asking God for insight as you study. You can pray for specific requests at the end of the meeting, or stop momentarily to pray if a particular situation comes up during your discussion. Then begin your time together by using the following questions and activities to get people talking:

- What has surprised you most about this group? Where did God meet you over the past six weeks?

- How have you seen new technology change the way you relate, think, and live?

- Take some time for each person to share about how they've done with inviting the people on the Circles of Life to church or your small group. What specific conversations are you praying about for the weeks to come?

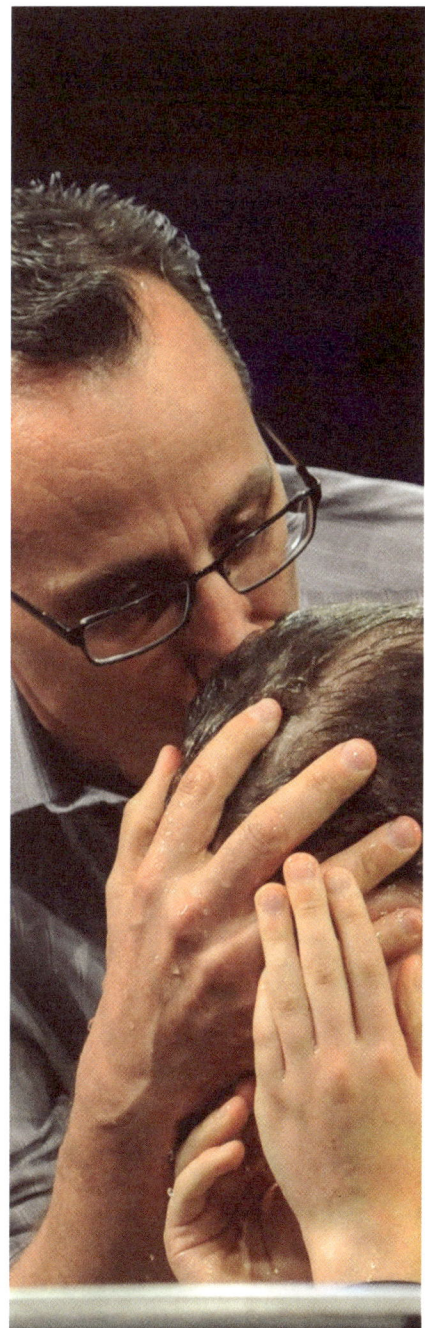

WATCH THE VIDEO

Use the space provided to record your thoughts and questions as well as the things you want to remember or follow up on. After watching the video, have someone read the discussion questions in the Hear God's Story section and start the conversation.

1 CORINTHIANS 9:24-27

Do you not know that in a race all the runners run, but only one gets the prize? Run in such a way as to get the prize. Everyone who competes in the games goes into strict training. They do it to get a crown that will not last, but we do it to get a crown that will last forever. Therefore I do not run like someone running aimlessly; I do not fight like a boxer beating the air. No, I strike a blow to my body and make it my slave so that after I have preached to others, I myself will not be disqualified for the prize.

THINK ABOUT IT

- What is this race about?

- What is the prize that Paul is referring to?

- In your own words, what did Paul mean when he said, "No, I strike a blow to my body and make it my slave so that after I have preached to others, I myself will not be disqualified for the prize."?

- How might this passage relate to the way we approach technology?

STUDY NOTES

The race that Paul is talking about is about spreading the good news of Jesus Christ. We are not only invited to watch the game, but we are called to be part of it. This race is not just a race to prove right from wrong, but it is a race of life or death: *"Fight the good fight of the faith. Take hold of the eternal life to which you were called when you made your good confession in the presence of many witnesses."* (**1 Timothy 6:12**). Fight off the distractions that keep you from reaching the goal. Instead of being distracted by technology, use it to win the race and spread the gospel.

CREATE A NEW STORY

In this section, talk about how you will apply the wisdom you've learned from the teaching and Bible study. Then think about practical steps you can take in the coming week to live out what you've learned.

- Can you think of a time when technology kept you from being fully present for something important, or when you missed out on real life because you were distracted by the digital world? What did you miss out on?

- Do you feel that your approach to technology is aimless or purposeful? Why?

- What are some ways you've tried to be purposeful with technology? Has it worked?

- If your group still needs to make decisions about continuing to meet after this session, have that discussion now. Talk about what you will study, who will lead, and when you will meet.

- Review your Small Group Agreement on page 112 and evaluate how well you met your goals. Discuss any changes you want to make as you move forward.

- Close by praying for your prayer requests and take a couple of minutes to review the praises you have recorded over the past six weeks on the Prayer and Praise Report on page 118. Spend some time thanking God for all He's done in your group during this study.

FOR ADDITIONAL STUDY

Take some time between now and your next meeting to dig into God's Word. Explore the Bible passages related to this session's theme on your own. Jot down your reflections in a journal or in this study guide. You may want to use a Bible website or app to look up commentary on these passages. If you would like, share what you learn with the group during your next meeting.

COLOSSIANS 3:16-17

Let the message of Christ dwell among you richly as you teach and admonish one another with all wisdom through psalms, hymns, and songs from the Spirit, singing to God with gratitude in your hearts. And whatever you do, whether in word or deed, do it all in the name of the Lord Jesus, giving thanks to God the Father through him.

- Take a moment to meditate on these verses.
- Do you fill yourself with God's word? Or do you fill yourself with other things?
- How do you praise God?
- What are you thankful for?

ROMANS 10:14-15

How, then, can they call on the one they have not believed in? And how can they believe in the one of whom they have not heard? And how can they hear without someone preaching to them? And how can anyone preach unless they are sent? As it is written: "How beautiful are the feet of those who bring good news!"

- How can this passage relate to the topic of technology?
- Have you been preaching the good news?
- Has "screen time" distracted you from ministering to others?
- With technology in mind, how can you fulfill this verse: *"How beautiful are the feet of those who bring good news!"*.

105

DAILY DEVOTIONS

DAY 1

1 CORINTHIANS 10:31-33

So whether you eat or drink or whatever you do, do it all for the glory of God. Do not cause anyone to stumble, whether Jews, Greeks or the church of God—even as I try to please everyone in every way. For I am not seeking my own good but the good of many, so that they may be saved.

REFLECT

Whatever you do, do it for the glory of God. However you use your screen time, are you honoring God with it? Are you watching things that bring you closer to God, or further away? What kind of thoughts are triggered when you are on social media?

DAY 2

ECCLESIASTES 1:9

What has been will be again, what has been done will be done again; there is nothing new under the sun.

REFLECT

What do you think this verse means? Re-write it in your own words.

DAY 3

1 CORINTHIANS 6:12

"I have the right to do anything," you say—but not everything is beneficial. "I have the right to do anything"—but I will not be mastered by anything.

REFLECT

Are you the master of your choices, or are your choices owning you? Be sensitive to your heart and obey your God.

DAY 4

1 KINGS 19:12

After the earthquake came a fire, but the Lord was not in the fire. And after the fire came a gentle whisper.

REFLECT

Do you hear God's voice in your life? Or is your life so noisy that you can't hear Him? What do you need to change so you can hear God's voice?

DAY 5

1 PETER 5:10

And the God of all grace, who called you to his eternal glory in Christ, after you have suffered a little while, will himself restore you and make you strong, firm and steadfast.

REFLECT

We all need God's constant grace and forgiveness. There may have been a time that you misused technology in particular, but know that Christ forgives you and wants to give you full restoration. Paul wrote, "My grace is sufficient for you, for my power is made perfect in weakness.' Therefore I will boast all the more gladly about my weaknesses, so that Christ's power may rest on me." **(2 Corinthians 12:9)**.

DAY 6

REFLECT

Use the following space to reflect on what you learned this week and what God is saying to you.

APPENDICES
Resources to make your small group experience even better!

FAQ

WHAT DO WE DO ON THE FIRST MEETING OF OUR GROUP?
Like all fun things in life—have a party! A "get to know you" coffee, dinner, or dessert is a great way to launch a new study. You may want to review the Small Group Agreement 112 and share the names of a few friends you can invite to join you. But most importantly, have fun before your study time begins.

CAN WE DO THIS STUDY ON OUR OWN?
Absolutely! This may sound crazy, but one of the best ways to do this study is not with a full house but with a few friends. You may choose to gather with another couple or a few friends who would enjoy going out for dinner and then walking through this study.

WHAT IF THIS GROUP IS NOT WORKING FOR US?

You're not alone! This could be the result of a personality conflict, life stage difference, geographical distance, level of spiritual maturity, or any number of things. Relax. Pray for God's direction, and at the end of this study, decide whether to continue with this group or find another. However, don't bail out before the six weeks are up—God might have something to teach you. Also, don't run from conflict or prejudge people before you have given them a chance. God is still working in your life, too!

WHO IS THE LEADER?

Most groups have an official leader. But, ideally, the group will mature and members will rotate leadership of meetings. Healthy groups often rotate hosts and leaders on a regular basis. This model ensures that all members grow, give their unique contribution, and develop their gifts.

HOW DO WE HANDLE THE CHILDCARE NEEDS IN OUR GROUP?

Very carefully. Seriously, this can be a sensitive issue. We suggest that you empower the group to openly brainstorm solutions. You may try one option that works for a while and then adjust over time. One approach is for adults to meet in the living room or dining room and to share the cost of a babysitter (or two) who can watch the kids in a different part of the house. This way, parents don't have to be away from their children all evening when their children are too young to be left at home. A second option is to use one home for the children and a second home (close by or a phone call away) for the adults. A third idea is to rotate the responsibility of providing a lesson or caring for the children. This can be an incredible blessing for children. Finally, the most common solution is to decide that you need to have a night to invest in your spiritual lives individually or as a couple and to make your own arrangements for childcare. No matter what decision the group makes, the best approach is to dialogue openly about both the problem and the solution.

SMALL GROUP AGREEMENT

OUR PURPOSE: To provide an environment where participants experience authentic community and spiritual growth.

OUR VALUES:

GROUP ATTENDANCE	To give priority to the group meeting. We will call or email if we will be late or absent. (Completing the Small Group Calendar will minimize this issue).
SAFE ENVIRONMENT	To create a safe place where people can be heard and feel loved. (Please, no quick answers, snap judgments, or simple fixes).
RESPECT DIFFERENCES	To be gentle and gracious to fellow group members with different spiritual maturity, personal opinions, temperaments, or "imperfections." We are all works in progress.
CONFIDENTIALITY	To keep anything that is shared strictly confidential and within the group, and to avoid sharing improper information about those outside the group.
ENCOURAGEMENT FOR GROWTH	To be not just takers but givers of life. We want to spiritually multiply our life by serving others with our God-given gifts.
SHARED OWNERSHIP	To remember that every member is a minister and to ensure that each attender will share a small team role or responsibility over time.
ROTATING HOSTS / LEADERS & HOMES	To encourage different people to host the group in their homes and to rotate the responsibility of facilitating each meeting. (See the Small Group Calendar).

SMALL GROUP CALENDAR

MEETING DATE	LESSON NUMBER	HOST HOME	MEAL OR DESSERT	GROUP LEADER
MONDAY JAN. 15	1	STEVE & LAURA'S	JOE	BILL

MEMORY VERSES

SESSION ONE

Very early in the morning, while it was still dark, Jesus got up, left the house and went off to a solitary place, where he prayed.

Mark 1:35

SESSION TWO

Whatever you do, work at it with all your heart, as working for the Lord, not for human masters...

Colossians 3:23

SESSION THREE

The Lord will guide you always; he will satisfy your needs in a sun-scorched land and will strengthen your frame. You will be like a well-watered garden, like a spring whose waters never fail.

Isaiah 58:11

SESSION FOUR

The wise store up choice food and olive oil, but fools gulp theirs down.

Proverbs 21:20

SESSION FIVE

I press on toward the goal to win the prize for which God has called me heavenward in Christ Jesus.

Philippians 3:14

SESSION SIX

Remember the Sabbath day by keeping it holy.

Exodus 20:8

SMALL GROUP LEADERS

Key resources to help your leadership experience be the best it can be.

PRAYER AND PRAISE REPORT

	PRAYER REQUEST	PRAISE REPORT
SESSION 1		
SESSION 2		
SESSION 3		
SESSION 4		
SESSION 5		
SESSION 6		

SMALL GROUP ROSTER

NAME	EMAIL	PHONE #

HOSTING AN OPEN HOUSE

If you're starting a new group, try planning an open house before your first formal group meeting. Even if you have only two to four core members, it's a great way to break the ice and to consider prayerfully who else might be open to joining you over the next few weeks. You can also use this kick-off meeting to hand out study guides, spend some time getting to know each other, discuss each person's expectations for the group, and briefly pray for each other. A simple meal or good desserts always make a kick-off meeting more fun.

After people introduce themselves, have everyone respond to a few icebreaker questions:

- What is your favorite family vacation?
- What is one thing you love about our church / our community?
- What are three things about your life growing up that most people here don't know?

Next, ask everyone to tell what he or she hopes to get out of this study. You might want to review the Small Group Agreement and talk about each person's expectations and priorities.

Finally, set an open chair (maybe two) in the center of your group and explain that it represents someone who would enjoy or benefit from this group but who isn't here yet. Ask people to pray about inviting someone to join the group over the next few weeks. Hand out postcards and have everyone write an invitation or two. Don't worry about ending up with too many people; you can always have one discussion circle in the living room and another in the dining room after you watch the lesson. Each group could then report prayer requests and progress at the end of the session.

You can skip this kick-off meeting if your time is limited, but you'll experience a huge benefit if you take the time to connect with each other in this way.

LEADING FOR THE FIRST TIME

SWEATY PALMS ARE A HEALTHY SIGN
The Bible says that God is gracious to the humble. Remember who is in control; the time to worry is when you're not worried. Those who are soft in heart (and sweaty-palmed) are those whom God is sure to speak through.

SEEK SUPPORT
Ask your leader, co-leader, or close friend to pray for you and prepare with you before the session. Walking through the study will help you anticipate potentially difficult questions and discussion topics.

BRING YOUR UNIQUENESS TO THE STUDY
Lean into who you are and how God wants you to uniquely lead the study.

PREPARE. PREPARE. PREPARE.
Go through the session several times. If you are using the video, listen to the teaching segment and Host Lifter. Don't wait until the last minute to prepare!

ASK FOR FEEDBACK SO YOU CAN GROW
Perhaps in an email or on cards handed out at the study, have everyone write down three things you did well and one thing you could improve on. Don't get defensive. Instead, show an openness to learn and grow.

PRAYERFULLY CONSIDER LAUNCHING A NEW GROUP
This doesn't need to happen overnight, but keep growth as a goal. Not all Christians are called to be leaders or teachers, but we are all called to be "shepherds" of a few someday.

SHARE WITH YOUR GROUP WHAT GOD IS DOING IN YOUR HEART
God is searching for those whose hearts are fully his. Share your trials and victories. We promise that people will relate.

LEADERSHIP TRAINING

Congratulations! You have responded to the call to help lead your group. As you prepare to lead, whether it is one session or the entire series, here are a few thoughts to keep in mind.

- Remember that you are not alone. It is common for good leaders to feel they are not ready to lead. Moses, Solomon, Jeremiah, and Timothy were all reluctant to lead. God promises, *"Never will I leave you; never will I forsake you."* (**Hebrews 13:5**). Whether you are leading for one evening, for several weeks, or for a lifetime, you will be blessed as you serve.

- Don't try to do it alone. Pray right now for God to help you build a healthy leadership team. If you can enlist a co-leader to help you lead the group, you will find your experience to be much richer. This is your chance to involve as many people as you can in building a healthy group. All you have to do is call and ask people to help. You'll probably be surprised at the response.

- Just be yourself. If you won't be you, who will? God wants you to use your unique gifts and temperament. Don't try to do things exactly like another leader; do them in a way that fits you! Just admit it when you don't have an answer, and apologize when you make a mistake. Your group will love you for it, and you'll sleep better at night!

- Prepare for your meeting ahead of time. Review the session and the leader's note, and write down your responses to each question. Pay special attention to exercises that ask group members to do something other than engage in discussion. These exercises will help your group live out what the Bible teaches, not just talk about it. Be sure you understand how an exercise works, and bring any necessary supplies (such as paper and pens) to your meeting. If the exercise employs one of the items in the appendix, be sure to look over that item so you'll know how it works. Finally, review the Outline for Each Session so you'll remember the purpose of each section in the study.

- Pray for your group members by name. Before you begin your session, go around the room in your mind and pray for each member by name. You may want to review the prayer list at least once a week. Ask God to use your time together to touch the heart of every person uniquely. Expect God to lead you to whomever He wants you to encourage or challenge in a special way. If you listen, God will surely lead!

- When you ask a question, be patient. Someone will eventually respond. Sometimes people need a moment or two of silence to think about the question. If silence doesn't bother you, it won't bother anyone else. After someone responds, affirm the response with a simple "thanks" or "good job." Then ask, "How about somebody else?" or "Would someone who hasn't shared like to add anything?" Be sensitive to new people or reluctant members who aren't ready to say, pray, or do anything. If you give them a safe setting, they will blossom over time.

- Provide transitions between questions. When guiding the discussion, always read aloud the transitional paragraphs and the questions. Ask the group if anyone would like to read the paragraph or Bible passage. Don't call on anyone, but ask for a volunteer, and then be patient until someone begins. Be sure to thank the person who reads aloud.

- Break up into smaller groups each week. If your group has more than seven people, we strongly encourage you to have the group gather at times in discussion circles of three or four people during the Hear God's Story or Create a New Story sections of the study. With a greater opportunity to talk in a small circle, people will connect more with the study, apply what they're learning quicker, and ultimately get more out of it. A small circle also encourages a quiet person to participate and tends to minimize the effects of a more vocal or dominant member. When you gather again